BOOKBINDING AT

A fully illustrated stage-by-stage guide to t
materials and tools are needed, and descriptior

BOOKBINDING AT HOME

The Basics of Bookbinding Simply Explained in Words and Diagrams

by
K. Riberholt and A. Drastrup
Translated from the Danish by Anthony Hopkinson

THORSONS PUBLISHERS LIMITED
Wellingborough, Northamptonshire

First published in Denmark as
Indbinding af boger

© 1978 by Clausen Boger, Kobenhavn
First published in England 1980
Second Impression May 1981
Third Impression November 1981

© THORSONS PUBLISHERS LIMITED 1980

ISBN 0 7225 0575 2 (hardback)
ISBN 0 7225 0598 1 (paperback)

Photoset by Harper Phototypesetters, Northampton.
Printed in Great Britain by
King's English Bookprinters Limited, Bramley, Leeds,
and bound by Weatherby Woolnough,
Wellingborough, Northamptonshire.

D
686.302
RLB

CONTENTS

FOREWORD

As a papermaker, I have been interested in bookbinding for many years, and I am familiar with a good number of the books which have been published on the subject. Most of them leave a lot to be desired. Some are just not very well written and others make the subject so complicated that they put it beyond the reach of beginners.

I was therefore delighted to see this book when it first arrived from Denmark. Here at last was a well thought out description of the basics of bookbinding with simple, clear illustrations. The book does not demand a large range of complicated, specialist equipment; it recommends only the essential tools, some of which can be made at home.

Naturally, such a book does not set out to be a complete account of an ancient and highly skilled craft. When you have read it you will not be able to go out and rival the masters who have had years of training and even more years of experience. You will, though, be able to make a fair job of binding some of your own favourite books. (Some of the techniques described are not common practice in Britain but there's no great harm in that.)

One word of warning. The techniques for repairing books described here are generally sound but no one should attempt to use them on old or valuable books without seeking advice from an expert.

ANTHONY HOPKINSON
(Author of *Papermaking at Home**)

* Published by Thorsons Publishers Limited in 1978.

1
MATERIALS AND TOOLS FOR BOOKBINDING

Materials

Before you start to bind a book you must decide what colour or combination of colours you are going to use for the cover, edges, endpapers and spine, and whether you are going to use paper, cloth or leather. The style of the spine must also be considered: how will the title be laid out and what colour will the title label be? In short, you must make a careful plan before starting, rather than letting the result depend on how things turn out in the end.

The various materials are best obtained from specialist suppliers of bookbinding materials, as they will have the widest range to choose from. There is a short list of suppliers in Britain at the end of the book.

Printing Paper

There are many different sorts of paper used for the printing of books: rag paper, chemical wood pulp or mechanical wood pulp, thick or thin, soft or hard. The characteristic of the paper can play a big part in selecting the right treatment for the book. If the paper, for example, is thin and hard, while the book has many pages, a thin thread must be used for sewing the sections. If the paper is thick and soft a thicker thread must be used. The soft paper is also more difficult to trim and you must take the greatest care when dealing with the edges of the book.

You must also discover the grain direction of the paper used in the book for this has a bearing on the joints between the front and back boards and the spine (see page 52).

Newspaper

This is used as an underlay during pasting and gluing operations.

Kraft Paper

This is very strong packaging paper, made from sulphate pulp. It comes in various qualities and thicknesses, either in rolls or sheets. It is used to pack the spine and make it smooth. (It can also be used to build up the thickness of the boards to suit the joint of the book.)

White Paper (Bank Paper)

Sometimes you can use a piece of white bank paper to separate the flysheet and a coloured end paper. If, though, the paper used in the book is lightly tinted it is best not to use it since its white colour would make too much of a contrast.

Bank paper is also used to repair the sections of the book. For this purpose it is important to find the correct grain direction, especially when it is used to strengthen the spine of a section.

End papers
These papers are available in many different qualities and types. They can be patterned on one side or both. Both sides can have a smooth texture or one can have a rough surface. In the latter case, it is the smooth surface which is stuck to the cover boards. If the end paper has a printed pattern the reverse is often marked and must be backed with bank paper.

Cover Papers
These too are found in many different qualities and types, from the cheapest printed papers to the more expensive hand coloured papers. By using high grade cover papers you can enhance the appearance of your books and give them a special interest.

If you cannot find ready-made paper which goes with the spine material and is in harmony with the book's contents you can make your own paper with an appropriate pattern or motif. You can print this for yourself with lino or potato cuts.

Board
The most suitable board for bookbinding is grey in colour and is either fibre-board or, best of all, millboard. White board should be avoided because it breaks very easily, and so should strawboard except for your less important work.

Glazed paper
This is strong, shiny paper, made from flax and hemp. It can be bought in sheets. It is used next to freshly glued or pasted sheets to prevent the moisture of the adhesive from spreading to other parts of the book.

Cord
This is usually made from hemp and is bought in balls, reels or cards. It comes in various thicknesses and can even be used doubled on the thickest books.

Thread
This is made from flax or hemp. The latter is best and is usually waxed. The advantages of using waxed thread are that it runs more smoothly, is less likely to cut the paper and does not absorb moisture from glue or paste. Like cord, it can be bought in balls, reels or cards and is available in various thicknesses.

Jaconette
This is a gauze-like cotton material. The name is probably a corruption of the Indian place name Jagganath. The material is bought in metre lengths and cut into strips for reinforcing end papers.

Tape
Tape is used instead of cord for the sewing of notebooks, photograph albums and other books which need to open up well at the spine; for the same reason, such books do not have a joint beaten in.

Tape can be bought in various widths, the widest being used for the thickest books. The widths most generally used are between 1 cm ($\frac{3}{8}$ inch) and 2½ cm (1 inch). Strips of spine covering material can be used instead of tape.

Headbands

Headbands are strips of woven linen or silk which are glued to the head and foot of the spine of a book for decoration. The material is obtainable in metre lengths, either single or double. The double variety has the decorative weave running from edge to edge of the strip so that it has to be cut in half lengthwise before use.

In place of headband material a strip of thin leather, doubled over, can be used.

Paste

Wallpaper adhesive, bought from a hardware store, can be used for paste. It has the consistency of thick porridge and is thinned with cold water before use. This type of paste can be kept without it going mouldy, as the makers add preservatives to it. It can also be bought in powder form to be mixed with cold water. First put the water in a container and then add the powder, a little at a time, so that it mixes rapidly. Note carefully the instructions for various processes in this book to see whether paste or glue should be used for a particular operation.

Glue (PVA adhesive)

PVA adhesive is a runny, milk-like substance. It dries quickly and is very flexible. Nowadays it is widely used in professional binderies as well as by amateurs. Gelatine glues, made from boiled animal bones, were traditionally used; they have to be heated in a glue pot and kept hot during work so they are more trouble than PVA or modern cold starch glues but they should always be used for old or valuable books.

Colours

Colours for decorating the edges of books are usually aniline dyes, which are water soluble. They can be mixed together or used one after another.

Wax

The best quality is beeswax, bought in cakes. It is used for waxing threads and for polishing the edges of books after the application of colour. If the blade in the plough is waxed before use it will be less hard on sensitive papers.

Chalk

This is ordinary blackboard chalk, bought in sticks. It can be used to decorate the edges of books.

Bookcloth

A closely woven cotton material. There are many different types, including imitation leather which is produced by giving the cloth a special coating and impressing this coating with a pattern like the grain of leather. Bookcloth is a strong material, easy to use and available in lengths in many different colours.

Linen

Linen is available in many different qualities and strengths and is used as a covering material.

Leather

Leather is the foremost, finest and most durable of materials for binding books. It is animal hide, treated in a special way. Leather intended for shoes, handbags etc. is no good for bookbinding.

Leather has a flesh side and a hair side, or grain, which is characteristic of each of the many different types. Particularly thick skin is sliced on a machine. The hair side is the better and stronger. The other side is called skiver and is provided with an artificial grain.

Some leather is double sided; you can discover this when you rub the leather with your hands: the two sides will separate in places and form bubbles or blisters. These defects cannot be put right so such material is unsuitable. When cutting the leather for the spine one must use the length, head to tail. The leather from the animal's back is the strongest, so this is preferred for the spine of the book, while the leather coming from closer to the belly is suitable for the corners.

Here are a few of the many different types of leather appropriate for bookbinding:

Sheepskin is entirely smooth. It is the cheapest leather and also the least durable.

Calfskin is a soft, strong leather with a smooth surface. It is ideal for bookbinding. It is a little heavier than some other types and is easily scratched.

Goatskin is also a soft and strong leather, easy to pare and perhaps the finest of all. It goes under a variety of names, according to its origin, for example morocco, niger, levant, shagreen etc. To avoid damaging the texture the material must not be pressed too hard when it is damp.

Vellum this material was once used for books and manuscripts before paper became common. It can also be used as a covering material. It is made from various skins, such as ass, goat, calf and sheep. The material is not tanned, as with other leathers, but treated with lime. It can be used to cover the corners although some other material may have been used for the spine.

Russian leather is made of calf-skin tanned in birch oil, which gives it a particularly pleasant fragrance.

Sharkskin is hard-wearing and does not show scratches and marks. The grain is somewhat uneven and very hard so you cannot gild straight onto it. Consequently, a title label must be attached, made from a different leather.

Title leather this is material made specially thin and used for titles and volume numbers.

By and large, the rule is to choose a material for binding which is strong and has an even surface and suitable thickness.

Type for Book Titles
Whether you are going to letter the titles of your books yourself or get someone else to do it for you, a knowledge of type styles is necessary. You must plan where the title is to be placed and which typeface will be used so that it can harmonize with the general appearance and theme of the book. Type is made from a material specially made out of a mixture of lead, tin and antimony.

This drawing shows the names of the parts of a piece of type.

1.   Counter
2.   Hair line
3.   Serifs
4.   Face
5.   Bevel
6.   Beard
7.   Pin-mark
8.   Nick
9.   Groove
A-B Body size (depth)
C-D Set (width)
4.-10. Type height

Type is measured in 'points' not in millimetres or inches. The size of a point varies between countries. In Britain and the United States of America one point is 1/72 of an inch. Strictly speaking, the point size refers to the body of the type, not to the actual printing character. This example will give you an idea of the point sizes most generally used:

R	R	R	R	R
points: 6	8	9	10	12

The first printed book was in Gutenberg's Gothic or 'Black Letter' typeface but in about 1470 the Italians developed the style now called Roman. Typefaces, until the eighteenth century, followed the form known as Old-Face, which was succeeded by Transitional and Modern.

Old-Face: Serifs sloping and forming a wide curve where they join the stems of the letters. Not much contrast between thick and thin strokes.

Transitional: Serifs slope less:

Modern: Serifs at right angles to stems and without curves where they join the stems. Strong contrast between thick and thin strokes.

Typefaces, such as Grotesque, which have no serifs are called 'sans serif'.

Many typefaces are named after their designers, such as, for example: Garamond, Janson, Baskerville, Bodoni.

Garamond
Old-Face   Garamond

Janson
Baskerville   Janson
Transitional

Bodoni
Modern   **Bodoni**

Most type faces have an upright and an italic form and both of these are usually found in Bold, Medium and Light.

As well as letters, figures and symbols a fount of type, as it is called, includes spaces of various widths which are used to separate words from each other and to improve the appearance of a word by making fine spaces between some of the individual letters.

Tools
Here is a list of the tools generally used for bookbinding. You can make some of them for yourself if you are reasonably good with your hands. In addition to normal art materials you will need:

1. A set square.
2. A metal rule (and a wooden rule for leatherwork).
3. Two straight-edges.
4. A wooden or metal try square.
5. Screwdriver.
6. Square-headed hammer.
7. Pair of pliers.
8. Backing hammer.
9. Three-sided file, reasonably fine.
10. Fine-toothed saw, preferably a tenon saw.
11. Scissors, preferably book-binders' scissors.
12. A board-cutting knife (usually has a retractable blade).
13. A paper knife.
14. Paring knife. Available in many different forms, both with and without handle. If it has no handle you can make one by binding a piece of

leather or cloth round it. In order to keep a very sharp edge on this knife it should never be used for anything but paring leather.

15. Grindstone, usually made of carborundum.

16. Paring stone. You can use a discarded lithographic stone or a slab of marble. You can also use a small sheet of glass but make sure to bind the edges with adhesive tape.

17. Paste brush.

18. Two bone folders, one rounded at the end and the other pointed.

19. A sprinkler. You can use an ordinary sieve as a substitute.

20. A stiff brush. You can use a nail brush or toothbrush.

21. Small sponge.

22. A fraying plate. You can make it yourself from a piece of zinc or brass. Bore a hole in the plate and cut a thin slot from the edge to this hole.

23. A bowl for colours, deep enough for the head of a paint brush to dip right into it.

24. Several pressing boards in various sizes. You can never have too many of these. As a rule, pressing boards are made from hardwood. To give extra strength some boards have the fore edge furnished with a piece of the hardest possible wood— usually oak. Pressing boards come in many different sizes, the most usual being 18×26cm ($7 \times 10\frac{1}{4}$ inches) and 22×30cm ($8\frac{1}{2} \times 12$ inches). When forming the joint of a book, it is not necessary to use genuine pressing boards (see page 63).

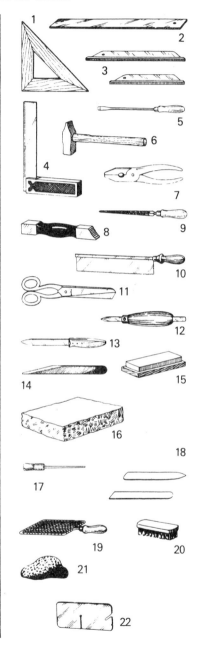

Knitting needles can be glued to boards made from thick ply-wood. The only important requirement for these boards is that they should be absolutely smooth. As an alternative to knitting needles you can use spokes from bicycle wheels.

25. A sewing frame. The model shown here takes apart for easy storage. One with threaded spindles has the advantage that all the threads can be slackened by the same amount at once by unscrewing the nuts supporting the crossbar. The trend is towards versions where the wooden spindles are replaced by metal ones.

26. Lying press. One with metal threads is preferable.

27. Key for the press.

28. Bookbinder's plough.

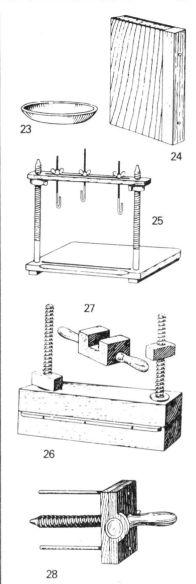

If you want to do good work you must observe precision and cleanliness and keep all your tools in good order. Pressing boards must be clean. Brushes must be well washed out so that paste and glue do not dry on them.

The most important thing of all is to keep your knives sharp with constant honing. Difficult sharpening, for example the honing of the round blade in the bookbinder's plough, is best left to an expert.

Knives which have to be particularly sharp, for example paring knives, should never be used for tasks other than those for which they are intended. Knife sharpening is usually done on a stone of marble or carborundum. Before using the stone, always put a few drops of oil on it.

2
PARTS OF A BOOK

.

Here is a list of terms used for the various parts of a book:

1. Fore edge.
2. Title page.
3. Half title.
4. Blank sheet of white paper ('white fly').
5. Flyleaf (sometimes coloured).
6. Corner.
7. End paper.
8. Front board or front cover.
9. Coloured cover paper.
10. Spine covering.
11. Tail.
12. Field between bands.
13. Raised bands.
14. Cerf (the edge of the spine next to the joint).
15. Spine.
16. Title label.
17. Tooling.
18. Head.
19. Headband.
20. Joint.
21. Turn-in.
22. Back board or back cover.
23. Edge.

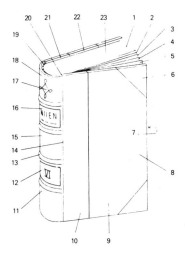

Inside the book the following terms are used:

1. Fly.
2. Backing for a coloured flyleaf ('White fly').
3. Coloured flyleaf.
4. End paper.
5. Flange.

Parts 1-5 are collectively called the end papers.

6. Jaconette strip.
7. End of cord.
8. Hollow spine.
9. Kraft lining for strengthening spine.
10. Headband.
11. Section.

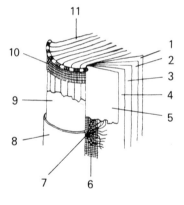

Methods of Binding

In general, there are three sorts of binding method, illustrated below:

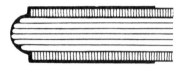

1. Rounded spine. No joint or hollow spine. The contents are attached to the spine covering.

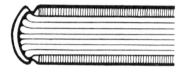

2. Rounded spine with a hollow. The joint is grooved, not filled by the cover bands.

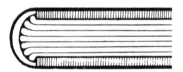

3. Rounded spine with a hollow. The cover boards fill in the joint.

Types of Binding

Quarter binding. When the spine is covered in a different material from the sides.

Half binding. When the spine and corners are covered in a different material from the sides.

Full binding. When the whole book is bound in one material. The term usually refers to books covered in leather.

Tight backed. Means a book without a hollow spine. It is usually quarter bound with a cloth spine and paper covered side boards.

Quarter bound book.

Full binding in cloth.   Full binding in paper.

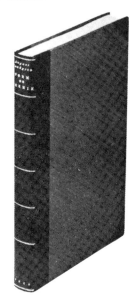

Half bound.   Half bound.

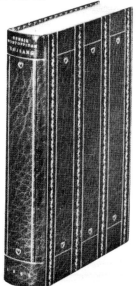

Full binding in leather.   Different types of spine decoration
                               on half bound books.

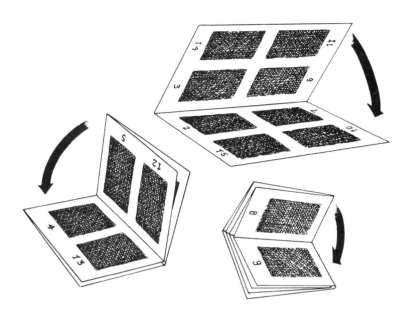

How a Book is Made Up

Many books are already sewn for binding, even if they have paper covers. A book consists of several large sheets called sections. The text is printed on the sheet so that there are eight blocks of type on each side. The section is folded along its middle (folio format) and so becomes two leaves with a total of four sides.

With the next fold there are four leaves with eight sides (quarto format). Finally a last fold gives eight leaves with sixteen sides (octavo format). This folding process means that the book's edges have to be cut before the pages can be read; usually this is done during the manufacture of the book. A book which is to be re-bound after much use may have the sections damaged in various ways; for instance, they may have been pulled askew at the spine. Great care has to be taken to keep the sections straight at the spine, though this is often difficult.

Many books are made up nowadays by a process called 'perfect binding'. After the sections have been folded and put together in order, the spine of the book is guillotined off so that at this stage the book consists of a number of loose sheets. Adhesive is applied to the spine, penetrating the edge of each sheet a little way to hold the book together. A book which has been perfect bound can be re-bound in the way described on page 87.

3
BINDING A BOOK

Now to show how to bind a book. We will begin by
going through the process of binding with a grooved
joint and a rounded spine with hollow. This basic
method will be followed by a description of other
methods of binding.

A book with grooved joints

Separating the Book
1. The cover of the book is removed with a horizontal pull.

3. After cutting the thread holding the first section, carefully pull the section free from the remainder of the book. Continue in the same way until you reach the last three sections. Often each section is numbered with an abbreviated version of the title of the book (see page 31 for an example).

2. When the book's sections are sewn, the thread must be cut. Usually a section consists of eight leaves (16 pages) and you will therefore find the thread showing at pages 8, 24, 40 et seq these being the centre pages of each section.

4. For the last three sections all threads are removed before you separate the sections one from another. This is because quite often the number of leaves in the last three sections varies.

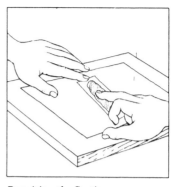

5. The remains of the old glue on the spine of each section are removed with a knife, taking care to avoid damaging the pages in any way.

Repairing the Sections

1. If any sections of the book are damaged they must be repaired. Tears in the text are mended with Japanese tissue. Paste is spread on a piece of tissue so that it does not reach right to the edges.

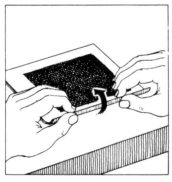

6. The curve which will have developed in the section while the book was being read can be corrected by bending back the spine of the section.

2. After the pasted strip of tissue has been placed over the tear in the paper and left to dry for six to eight hours, the part of the tissue which was left unpasted is torn carefully away.

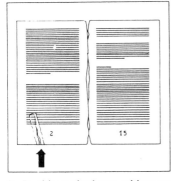

3. By this method you achieve an almost invisible join between the page of the book and the paper pasted on to repair it.

5. Using an underlay of newsprint, cut the paper into strips along the machine direction. The strips must be a little longer than the height of the book and about 12mm (½ inch) wide. While cutting the paper, hold the knife as shown so that the point will not tear the paper.

4. Repairs to the spine of the section are undertaken with a piece of bank paper. This paper must be tested for grain. All machine-made papers have the majority of their fibres running in one direction, the direction in which the paper ran on the machine when it was being formed. You can find the grain by pulling the edges of the paper between your finger and thumb. The edge which cockles less is the machine direction.

6. Put a strip onto a piece of newsprint and spread paste on one side of it.

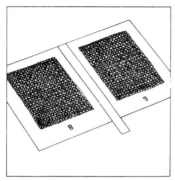

7. The strip should be laid onto the open section which is to be repaired in such a way that it is flush with the top of the section.

9. The fold should be well pressed either with a finger or a bone folder.

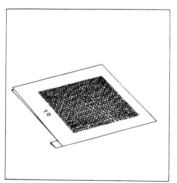

8. After the paste has dried for 5-10 minutes the section can be folded together.

10. The projecting edge of the strip is then cut away.

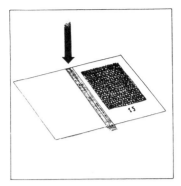

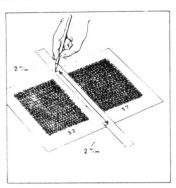

Reinforcing the Sections
1. The book can be reinforced by pasting a strip of linen onto the fold of the outermost leaf of the book's first and last sections. This is done in the manner already explained for repairing the sections.

Cutting out the Cover
1. Retain the cover if it is in harmony with the design of the book. Always keep it if the book is a first edition. Find the shortest leaf in the book and on a strip of paper make marks two millimetres short of the top and bottom of the book.

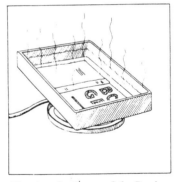

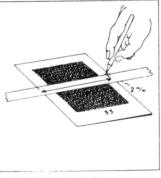

Cleaning the Cover of the Book
1. Dirt or yellow stains on the cover of a book can be cleaned by soaking the cover for a few minutes in bleaching liquid or a solution of detergent. The pan used for soaking the cover should be placed on a source of heat.

2. Similarly find the narrowest page in the book and on another strip of paper make a mark 2mm ($\frac{1}{10}$ inch) short of one edge.

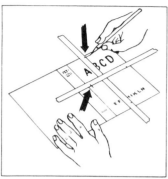

3. Lay the marked strips on the cover of the book and mark the cover at the top edge and spine as shown so that when the text is in the cover it will be a little nearer the spine than the fore edge and with a little more space at the bottom than at the top.

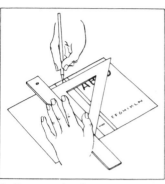

5. Draw cutting lines on the cover with the aid of a square and a ruler.

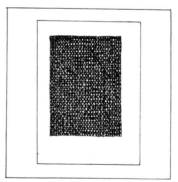

4. The type matter on a page is usually so placed that the distance from the text to each edge of the page differs. It is least to the spine, a little greater to the head, a little greater again to the fore edge and greatest of all to the foot of the page.

6. Lay the cover onto a paper waste underlay and cut along the line which runs across the spine and top edge. If you wish, you can wait until the rest of the binding work is complete before cutting the cover and inserting the contents.

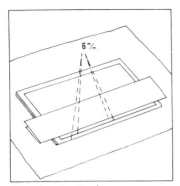

*Inserting the Contents
into the Cover*

1. Put the first section of the book on an underlay with the last page uppermost. On top of that place the cover, again with the back uppermost and set so that it lies 6mm (¼ inch) in from the spine of the section. Then put a strip of folded paper on the cover, about 6mm (¼ inch) in from the spine of the cover, as shown above.

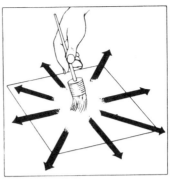

3. An exception to this rule is the pasting of large sheets. Here the strokes run from the centre out to the sides. This is necessary to avoid forcing the glue into the paper so that it affects the reverse side.

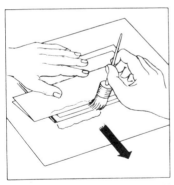

2. Now spread on paste. All pasting is done with a stroke which comes towards you.

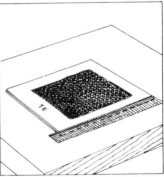

4. Remove the underlay and the cover. Cut a strip of linen so that it is just a little longer than the book and about 12mm (½ inch) wide, and press it hard onto the spine of the section so that it is flush with the top of the section.

5. Next bring the cover to the table with its inside uppermost, turn the section over and lay it on the cover as shown. Press the linen strip firmly and fold the cover over the section.

7. Cut away the overlapping part of the strip.

6. Press the strip well down with the fingers.

8. The back and spine of the cover are put back on the book as follows: Paste a piece of paper or cloth over the reverse of the spine. This must be big enough to give an overlap for gluing to the last section.

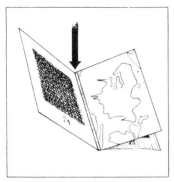

Putting in an Insert
1. Any insert is attached with a strip which is usually glued to the section or to one of its leaves. If the insert is to lie in the middle of the section you must spread a small edge of paste onto the back of the insert (indicated by hatching in the drawing) and attach it directly to the sheet.

3. Not every page in the book has to be numbered but on the front page of each section there usually appears the title and the number of the section (this is called the 'signature'). The next page in the section is sometimes marked with the same number with the addition of a star so that the two pages cannot be confused. Often the title is indicated in the signature by its initials only.

2. The pages in the repaired book can now be put together. Make sure that all the sections are in the correct order.

Pressing the Book
1. The book is stood on its upper edge and on its spine. Hold it with both hands in a loose grip and let the book fall under its own weight onto a table top. All the sections will then be aligned.

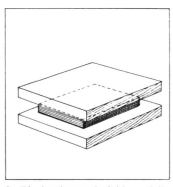

2. The book must be laid carefully on a pressing board with another board on top of it.

4. When the press is being tightened, you can exert extra pressure if you hold it between your knees with one end on the ground.

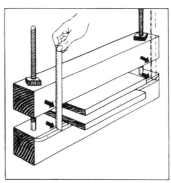

3. The whole book must then be put into a lying press which is then screwed up tightly. You must check with a rule to ensure that the press is screwed up an equal amount on each side; if not, damage can occur.

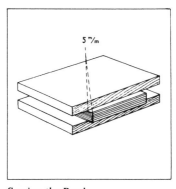

Sawing the Book
1. Take the book out of the press after it has stood for 10-12 hours. Remove the first and last sections and lay the rest between two boards so that the spine projects about 5mm ($\frac{1}{5}$ inch).

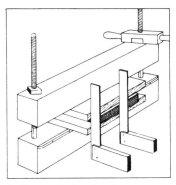

2. Return the book to the press and make sure that the spine is completely square, that the boards are exactly in line with each other and that all sections project an equal distance.

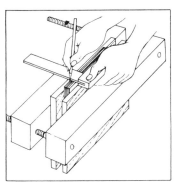

4. Put a final mark midway between the two inner marks. The sawcuts already in the book from the previous binding will also indicate the position for these marks. Extend all the marks across the book with the aid of a square held against the length of the spine.

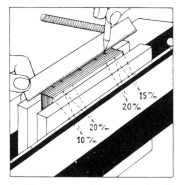

3. If you are working with a book of regular shape, make a mark 15mm (½ inch) from the foot of the book. Make another mark 10mm (⅖ inch) from the head of the book. Make two more marks each 20mm (¾ inch) from the first marks you inscribed.

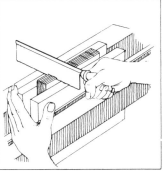

5. Saw along the lines you have drawn just deep enough to ensure that the saw edge penetrates the innermost leaf in each section.

6. So that the three innermost saw-cuts (or cerfs) are large enough for the binding cords to lie in them, use a file to open them to the right depth and breadth.

Making the End Papers
1. If the beginning of the book which is to be bound already has some blank sheets, use a single end paper. For this, cut a piece of paper as high as the book and two and a half times its breadth. Make sure that the paper is cut so that the grain runs from head to tail, not across the page.

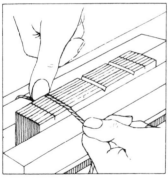

7. Each cerf must be filed deep enough to contain the thread but no deeper than necessary, otherwise it will be visible in the finished book and the book will become loose at the threads.

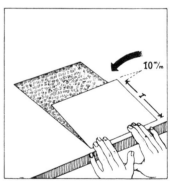

2. A piece of this paper 10mm (³⁄₅ inch) broader than the book is folded over so that the best side lies inwards.

3. Turn the sheet round and fold the outer piece over the part already folded. This small folded piece will be used as the flange for attaching to the cover boards.

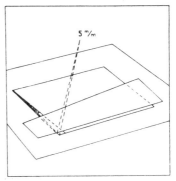

5. Now lay the end paper, with the flange folded inside, on a piece of paper and cover it with another piece of paper, folded once. This upper paper is placed so that 5mm ($\frac{1}{5}$ inch) of the end paper projects outside it.

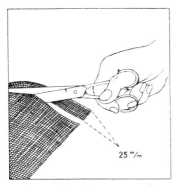

4. Cut a strip of jaconette as long as the height of the book and 25mm (1 inch) wide.

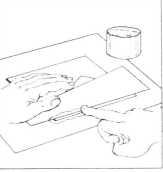

6. Spread this projecting edge with paste and remove the top paper and the underlay.

7. Press the jaconette strip firmly onto the end paper so that it sticks to the pasted edge.

9. Then the edge can be folded right back with the bone folder. This fold must not be made with too much pressure or the part which will eventually be inside the end paper might slip out.

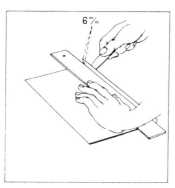

8. Now fold the end paper so that the flange lies outwards and lay it on the table with the flange downwards. On the edge to which the jaconette was attached, place a rule 6mm (¼ inch) from the edge and bend the paper up with a bone folder.

10. The end paper is now ready and if correctly made will appear like this.

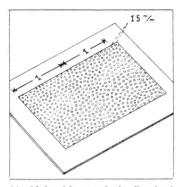

11. If the title page is the first leaf of the book a double end paper must be used. For this purpose cut out a piece of paper as high as the book and with a breadth twice that of the book plus 15mm (½ inch).

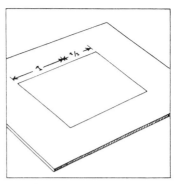

13. Then cut a piece of white bank paper according to its grain. This will be as high as the book and one and a half times its breadth.

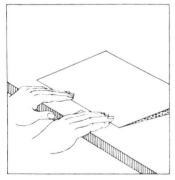

12. Fold the end paper in the middle so that the coloured face lies inwards.

14. Fold the white paper over the coloured end paper. The short piece of white paper is the flange.

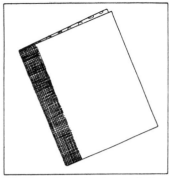

15. The coloured end paper is then folded together with the coloured side inwards, and a strip of jaconette should be pasted to the outer side of the fold.

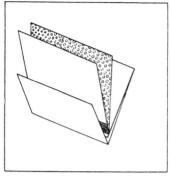

17. If the coloured end paper needs to be lined, because the colour shows through to the other side, take a piece of paper as high as the book and two and a half times its breadth. Fold this paper round the end paper, as shown, and fold the end papers as already described.

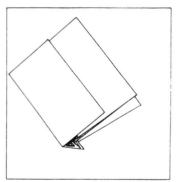

16. Lay the white paper outside the coloured end paper and fold the whole in the same way as for a single end paper. The double end paper now looks as above.

18. Whether the book is to have single or double end papers, make two sets and place the first and last sections of the book each into its own end paper.

19. Bring the end papers to the book, making sure that the flanges are on the outside. The book is now ready for sewing.

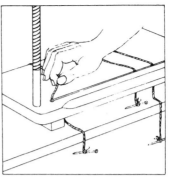

2. Pass the sewing cords through the slot in the bottom board of the sewing frame and secure the ends with a nail or something similar pulled up against the groove. Bend over the nail heads to avoid any risk of scratching the underside of the book which is being sewn.

Sewing the Book
1. Make marks for sewing on the fold of each end paper using one of the sections already sawn as a guide.

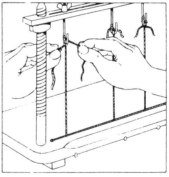

3. Next pull the cords up to the hooks at the top of the sewing frame, and make fast.

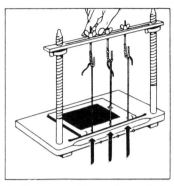

4. Place one of the sections of the book on the sewing frame and align the cords with the three innermost saw cuts, and tighten up with the aid of the wing nuts on top of the frame.

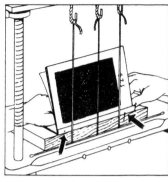

6. Take the last section to the sewing frame on a pressing board. Then pierce holes through the end paper and the section at the two outermost saw cut marks. The holes are pierced from the inside of the section outwards and they must be 2mm ($\frac{1}{10}$ inch) above the fold in the flange where they emerge.

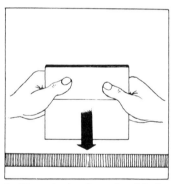

5. Place the book ready with the last section uppermost. The end paper with the last section inside should then be picked up and straightened at the top edge and spine.

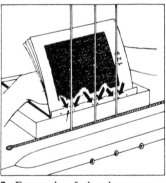

7. For each of the three centre sawcuts make two holes 2-3mm ($\frac{1}{10}$-$\frac{1}{8}$ inch) either side of the saw cut and again 2mm ($\frac{1}{10}$ inch) above the fold in the flange. More experienced bookbinders often prefer to sew directly without first making these guide holes.

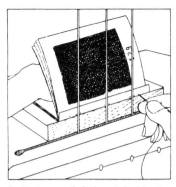

8. Put your left hand inside the centre of the section and with the right hand push the needle in through the first hole at the right hand end.

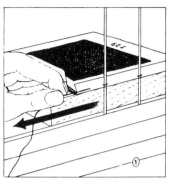

10. . . . until you reach the last hole in the section. The thread is tightened by pulling away from the book in a direction parallel with the spine.

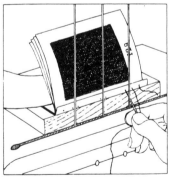

9. With your left hand pass the needle out through the next hole, pass it in the right hand over the vertical cord and push it in through the next hole. Continue in the same way . . .

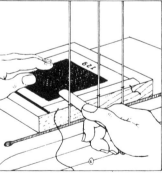

11. When you have finished sewing the section, press down well on the spine with a bone folder.

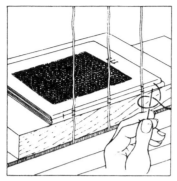

12. The last section but one is laid on top of the last section, and you sew through it, going back from left to right. Loosen the cords so that you can tighten the last section up well inside its end paper, and tie the thread to the loose end in the last section with two knots. Then tighten up the cords again.

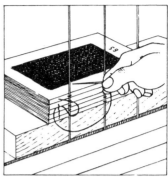

14. . . . after which the thread should be pulled tight.

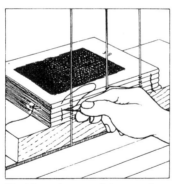

13. Now the remaining sections can be sewn. Each time you finish a section, pass the needle eye first between that section and the previous one . . .

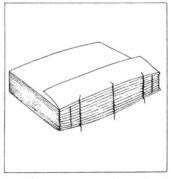

15. You must not pull too hard when pulling the thread between sections otherwise the book will be too tight at the ends.

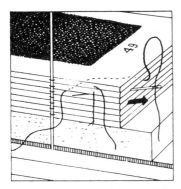

16. If you come to the end of the thread, a new length must be tied on. This must always be done at the end of a section. The needle with the new thread should be passed between the sections, as shown, with the eye first.

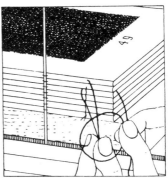

18. . . . meanwhile passing two fingers of the left hand through the loop and pulling the two loose ends back through. With a pull on the loop the knot automatically goes into the sawcut and the thread is joined with a double knot.

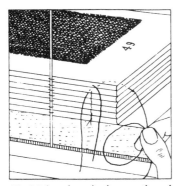

17. Make a loop in the new thread and hold it tightly with the right hand . . .

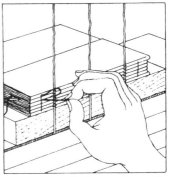

19. When sewing is over the needle should be passed between the second and third sections from the top, and the cords loosened.

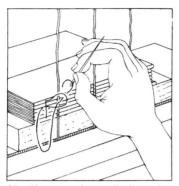

20. Then pass the needle through a loop in the third and pull it into a knot. Repeat the process to make a double knot.

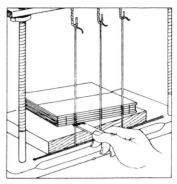

22. The book must not be sewn so tightly that it cannot be lifted up the cords with a bone folder.

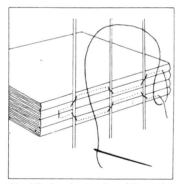

21. The book must be wider at the spine than at the fore edge. The thread used must have an appropriate thickness to achieve this. If the book is thick and printed on thin paper two sections can be sewn together as shown. The three final sections and the three first sections are always sewn singly.

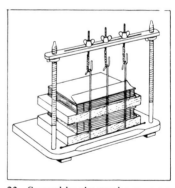

23. Several books can be sewn on the frame without changing the cords. Put a pressing board between each pair of books being sewn.

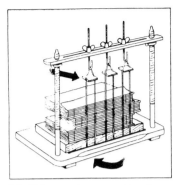

24. When sewing several books on the frame you can also use double cords, held apart at the top and bottom by small pieces of board, as shown. Use a different set of cords for each alternate book being sewn.

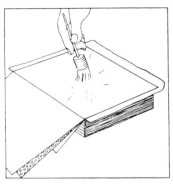

Lining the End Papers
1. If there is white paper in the end papers to line the coloured sheets the lining can now be carried out. Lay a piece of waste paper under the white paper. Then spread glue all over the white sheet. After gluing, remove the waste sheet, close up the book and put it in the press for a while.

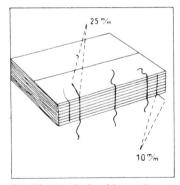

25. The book should now be cut free from the sewing frame, making sure that there is a 25mm (1 inch) length of free cord on either side of the book. All loose ends of the thread are cut back to 10mm (²⁄₅ inch).

Finishing the Sewing
1. When the book is dry again, put it back in the press with the spine projecting about 50mm (2 inches). Place pressing boards under the spine and knock down the swelling on each side of the book. Because this swelling has a part to play in the later stage of rounding the spine, it must not be knocked out completely.

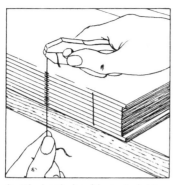

2. The book should now be laid on the edge of the table while you pull the cords tight, holding one end of each cord in the fingers and drawing the other end with a pair of pliers.

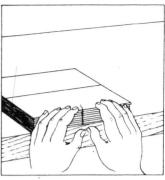

4. Close the book and stand it on its spine, and then press down on the book with your fingers.

3. The fold in the end paper should now be joined to the section by laying the book open on the edge of the table while the fold is spread with paste.

5. The cord ends should now be pulled tight in a fraying plate held in the left hand. The ends can be frayed with the back of a knife or a bone folder. The part of the cord closest to the spine can be scraped with a needle.

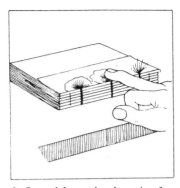

6. Spread the cord ends out in a fan shape and paste them to the flange so that they are as flat as possible.

2. Thin glue should be spread on the spine. The spreading is best done with strokes running from the middle of the spine outwards to the two ends.

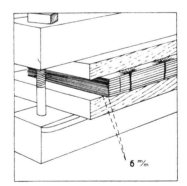

Gluing the Spine
1. Now put the book in the press with the spine projecting about 6mm (¼ inch). The press must not be tightened too much.

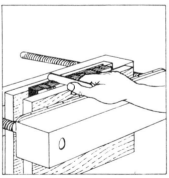

3. Press the glue well into the spine with a bone folder or the pane of a hammer.

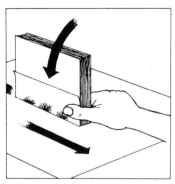

4. Knocking the spine down hard onto a piece of waste paper and pulling it rapidly along the paper will remove any surplus glue.

Cutting the Fore Edge
1. If the text is printed very close to the edges you will have to be content with cutting the top edge only. Otherwise, start with the fore edge as follows: Mark the breadth of the narrowest page on a strip of paper (see pages 27-28) and copy the marks onto the outside of the book.

5. After about 10 to 20 minutes the glue will be dry. It must not be allowed to set too hard before you continue work on the book. Take the book from the press and with several hammer blows force the first and last sections forwards. The rounding of the spine which results can be removed by standing the book on its spine.

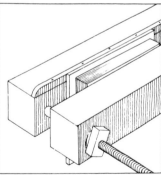

2. Now put the book into the press with the marks level with the top of the jaw of the press. A piece of board should be laid behind the book to protect the press during the cutting.

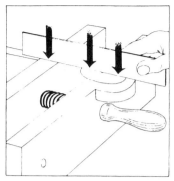

3. The blade of the plough must sit level, that is to say, it must align with a rule laid across the two sides of the plough.

5. Support the press as shown here when using the plough.

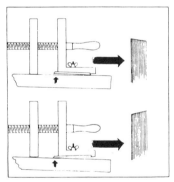

4. If the blade is askew, the book will be cut on a slant. The lie of the blade can be adjusted with a slip of paper placed under it. During work the blade must be well tightened so that it cannot slip round.

6. Hold the press against your body. The plough works from right to left and is held tight against the work and onto the jaw of the press. After every forward motion tighten the plough a little with the right hand on the return journey.

Rounding the Spine
1. When the fore edge has been planed, take the book from the press and lay it on the table. Open the book a little at the middle. Hold the upper part between first and second finger as shown, while pushing against the lower part of the book with the thumb.

3. At the end the book is completely closed; while keeping up a constant pull with the fingers, make the final rounding of the spine with the hammer.

2. While you pull on the book with the two fingers and push with the thumb, strike the spine lightly with a hammer. The book is handled thus several times on both sides. Each time it is turned over onto the other side, take fewer pages between the two fingers.

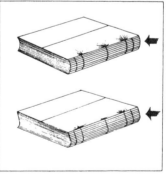

4. You must hold the book tightly as you turn it over, and if you have to stop work in the middle you must put a heavy weight on the book or the rounding will disappear. The spine must be evenly rounded; if it looks like the lower illustration it will be impossible to put in the joint later between the spine and the cover boards.

5. Minor irregularities in the cutting of the edges can be smoothed out with a piece of sandpaper wrapped round a piece of broom handle. For this operation the edge must be flush with the pressing boards and the pressing boards should be protected by two pieces of cardboard between them and the book.

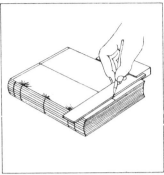

2. Rule lines from the marks and then cut the edges along these lines. Some people consider it an advantage to wait to cut the short edges until after the joint has been put in. There is no harm in doing this but it is important to take care when putting the book into the press to avoid damaging the joint.

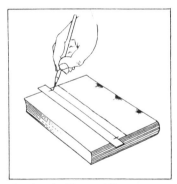

Cutting the Top and Bottom Edges of the Book
1. The length of the shortest page in the book was marked on a strip of paper (see page 27) and these marks are transferred to the outside of the book.

3. If you hold a rule against the edge of the book it should touch along the whole length if the book was correctly cut.

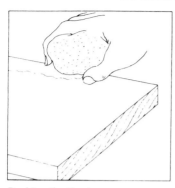

Backing the Book

1. This operation makes the joint into which the cover boards fit where they touch the spine. Moisten two pressing boards with a little water along their edges to prevent the book from moving while it is in the press.

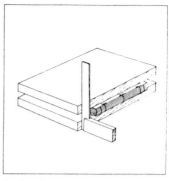

3. Book and pressing board should be turned over and another pressing board placed on top so that it lies back the same distance from the spine as the first board. Chalk the position of the two pressing boards with a set square.

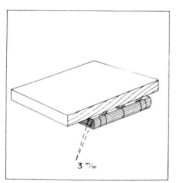

2. Lay one of these pressing boards on top of the book with the book projecting 1-4mm ($\frac{1}{32}$-$\frac{5}{32}$ inch). The thickness of the board to be used for the cover will determine the exact amount by which the book projects.

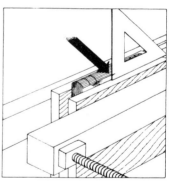

4. Put the whole assembly into the press and lightly tighten while carefully adjusting the position of the book by use of a set square pulled along next to the spine. Once the book is precisely lined up, fully tighten the press.

5. Knock down the joint with a hammer. Hold the hammer shaft parallel to the spine, and strike the sections of the book with light, curving blows. Begin where the rounding is highest but avoid striking the centre section since that would cause wrinkles in the book. Start knocking at the middle of the book and work outwards to the ends. The joint is knocked down until it rests on the pressing boards.

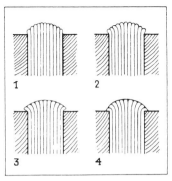

7. These drawings show how the sections are gradually forced into the form of the two joints. Great care must be taken as this is one of the stages in bookbinding where a mistake cannot afterwards be put right. After backing has been completed the book must remain in the press drying for 24 hours.

6. You can use a backing hammer; this is a tool specially made for this task, with its face cut into ridges. After backing one side of the book it is turned round and the other side backed in the same way.

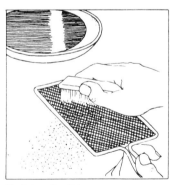

Staining the Edges
1. Put the book into the press. Pour a little colour or walnut stain into a pan, and with the help of a stiff brush and sprinkler (a sieve will do) the colour can be sprinkled onto the edges of the book.

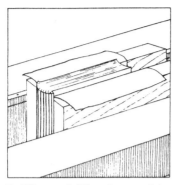

2. When sprinkling the top of the book put it between two boards arranged to protect the joints. To keep the press free from any colour which misses the book use two pieces of paper between the book and the press.

Putting on the Headband and the Hollow
1. The headband is not put on so that its top edge projects above the head of the book. It should be attached with glue and its length must be exactly the same as the width of the spine.

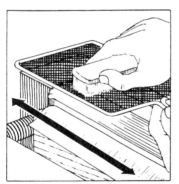

3. To apply the colour, load the brush and rub it across the surface of the sprinkler, at the same time moving the sprinkler along the length of the book.

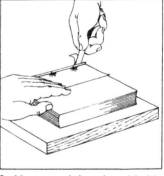

2. Next spread the spine with thin glue and lay a piece of kraft, stretching from one headband to the other but wider by 30-40mm (1¼-1½ inches) than the spine, along one joint and bent across the spine. The piece of the kraft which extends beyond the joint should be folded back, pressed with a bone folder and cut away with a paper knife.

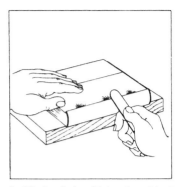

3. The kraft should then be rubbed well down with a bone folder.

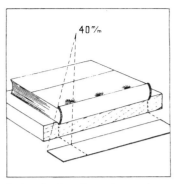

5. Mark the dimensions of the spine on a piece of thin board. The hollow will be made from this. It must be cut 40mm (1½ inches) longer than the spine. Bear in mind the grain of the board.

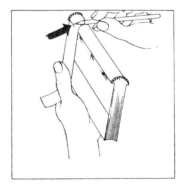

4. Measure the spine of the book both at the head and at the tail. The two measurements should be identical if the book has been correctly assembled.

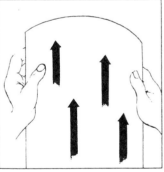

6. The grain or machine direction of the board can be found by rounding it in your hands. It will form a round more easily along the machine direction, since that is the way the fibres run.

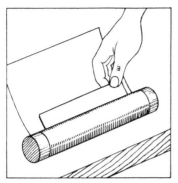

7. As every crease and irregularity will show in the finished book, the rounding of the board must be done with the greatest care. The best method is to wrap a piece of kraft round a round sectioned piece of wood of suitable diameter. Put the hollow inside the kraft, as shown.

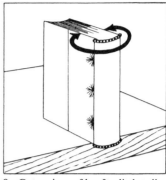

9. Cut a piece of kraft a little taller than the spine and as broad, as is shown in the drawing.

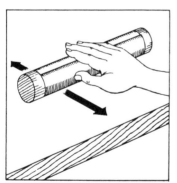

8. By rolling the wood back and forth you will round the hollow without damage.

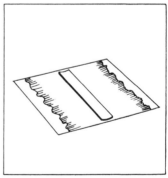

10. Spread paste on the kraft, without going right up to its edges, and lay the hollow in the middle.

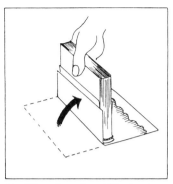

11. Place the spine of the book on the hollow and pull the kraft up against one side of the book.

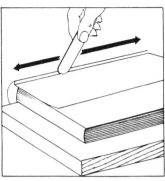

13. Lay the book on a pressing board so that the joint lies along the edge of the board. Press the upper part of the kraft paper with the end of a bone folder. Repeat for the other side of the book.

12. Pick up the book and hold it in your right hand. Use the fingers of the left hand to press down the kraft so that the hollow is in the correct position.

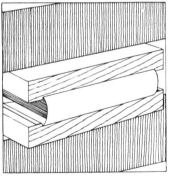

14. Once you are sure that the hollow is precisely in line with the spine, put the book between two pressing boards. The boards must be pushed right up against the joint so that the paper on either side of the hollow is pressed well into the joints. To prevent the book sticking to the pressing boards, put a piece of glazed paper on either side of the book.

15. When the book is quite dry, take it out of the press and tear off the part of the hollow paper which was left unglued. Rub the torn edge with fine sand paper so that the join will be as smooth as possible.

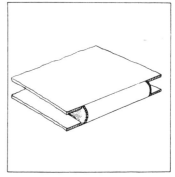

Putting On the Cover Boards
1. Take two boards of exactly the same thickness as the joint. In format these will be a little larger than the book itself. One edge, the edge to join the spine, must be trimmed so that it is completely straight.

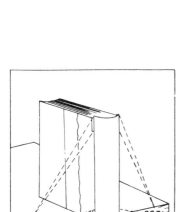

16. Four short cuts must now be made in the hollow at the joint, as shown. This is necessary so that later you can fold over the material used for covering the spine.

2. Rub a bone folder along the straight edge and then rub down with sandpaper. Some board has dark stripes down one face. These stripes must lie parallel to the spine of the book and the striped face must be inwards against the book itself. Make sure that the board has a little flexibility from spine to fore edge.

3. As you quite often have to use sandpaper it is a good plan to stick some to a piece of fairly thick board. Sandpaper can be stuck to both sides of the board, perhaps two pieces of different grades.

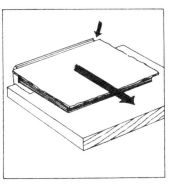

5. Lay the board on top of the book, keeping a gap between the board and the edge of the spine which is equal to half the thickness of the board. Repeat for the other side of the book.

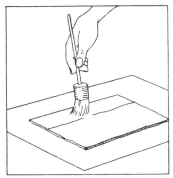

4. Now spread paste on a part of the board, just a little narrower than the flange.

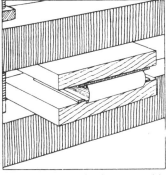

6. Put the book in the press with the spine facing outwards and the pressing boards reaching no further than the edges of the cover boards.

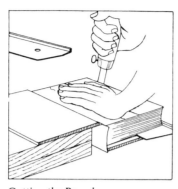

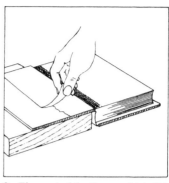

Cutting the Boards
1. After a day the boards can be cut so that they project a reasonable amount beyond the edges of the book. Use two rules, a narrower one for the top and bottom of the book and a broader one for the fore edge. Take care that the hollow is not damaged during the cutting of the boards.

3. The part of the flange which did not get pasted to the board should be torn off and its edge smoothed with sandpaper.

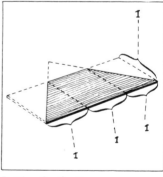

2. Cut the ends of the hollow so that it is the same length as the cover boards. This is done by letting one leg of the scissors rest on the edge of the boards, holding it steady with the thumb. When you make the cut the hollow will be the correct height. The edges of the boards are smoothed with a bone folder and sandpaper.

Putting On the Corners
of the Book
1. The corners of the book are cut out against a template, made from a piece of board with dimensions as shown above. The part of the spine material which extends over the front and back covers will have about the same measurement as the triangle of the corner.

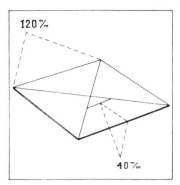

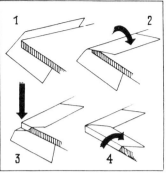

2. A template for the corners can also be formed from a square piece of board. Cut the corners along diagonals drawn across the board. For a book of average size a square with sides of 100-120mm (4 to 4¾ inches) will do. If the sides are 120mm (4¾ inches) the triangle for the corners will be 120mm × 60mm (4¾ × 2⅜ inches) but the top 20mm (¾ inch) of the triangle of material is cut off to leave the height at 40mm (1⅝ inches).

4. The corner should be folded first along the shorter edge and pressed down with a nail at the corner. Then the other side should be folded over the longer edge of the cover. Make sure you press the material well into the edges of the boards with a bone folder.

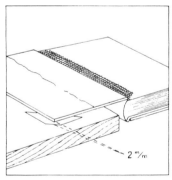

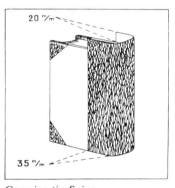

3. The corner should be spread with glue and laid on the cover so that the side which was cut short at the apex of the triangle projects 2mm (³⁄₃₂ inch) from the corner of the board. The side of the corner lying on the longer edge of the cover projects a little further than the one on the shorter edge.

Covering the Spine
1. Cut out a piece of material for the spine. The dimensions are a matter of taste, depending on how far you wish the material to reach across the front and back covers. We illustrate, by way of example, a piece which extends 35mm (1⅜ inch) across the covers. The material must be cut with 20mm (¾ inch) more height than the spine so that there is enough material to turn over.

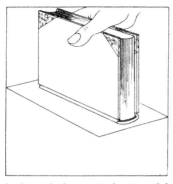

2. Spread glue onto the material and place the spine of the book on the material. Rub the material well down onto the spine by hand.

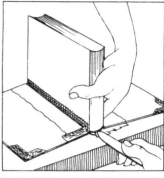

4. Lay the book spine down on the table. Hold the contents in the left hand while the right hand presses the edge of the spine covering onto the insides of the boards and the hollow. Use a bone folder and press really well.

3. Press the sides of the spine material well onto the boards and down into the joints. The material must also be pressed onto the edges of the boards.

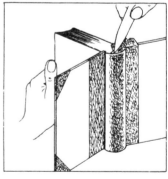

5. Some people prefer to hold the book in an upright position while they turn in the material. The book is placed on the edge of the table while the material is turned in at one end. Provided the book is held completely open, this method will work very well.

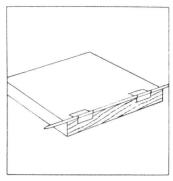

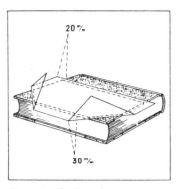

6. To give the joints a really good appearance, you can attach knitting needles or bicycle wheel spokes to the edges of a pair of pressing boards. The book should be put between the boards so that the needles lie in the joints. The book should then be pressed lightly for a short while. Once the spine is complete the book must not be handled for the next 24 hours.

Covering the Boards
1. The papers for the sides are cut so that they project 30mm (1¼ inch) beyond the fore edge and 20mm (¾ inch) beyond the top and bottom of the book. They are cut together from a piece of paper folded double with the face side inwards. Each paper is laid on the book and the corners folded in so that the paper overlaps the edge of the corner material by 2mm ($\frac{3}{32}$ inch).

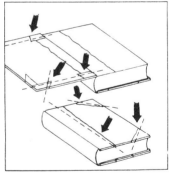

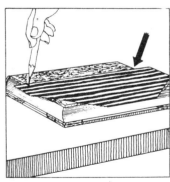

7. If the corners and the spine covering are slightly crooked, this can be put right now. The spine covering must be examined to make sure that it is the same width all the way from top to bottom and the corners must all be of equal size. Any irregularity can be corrected by cutting away the uneven edge with a knife. The turned over parts lying inside the boards are treated in the same way, as shown in the upper picture.

2. With a bone folder or pencil, make marks on the spine material an equal distance at top and bottom from the joint. The side paper, not yet glued, is laid down so that it covers the two marks equally. It must be positioned so that an equal amount of material shows at each corner. Then a pencil mark must be made on the side paper in line with the edge of the board forming the cover.

3. Now glue both pieces of paper. Allow the first piece to dry a little, then lay it on the board, as shown above, in line with the marks you made earlier. Do not use too thick a mixture of glue.

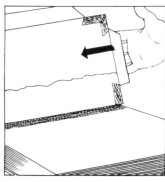

5. Turn over the edges of the paper with the hand and press down on the inside of the board. Start pressing the paper in the middle. If the turn in is too big, trim it to size. When the book is completely dry again, it is ready for end papering.

4. The paper should be smoothed out at the spine and corners. Use the fingers to do this, not a bone folder or the paper will become shiny.

End Papering
1. Trim the jaconette strip on the bias and lay a piece of waste paper under the end paper for protection. Take care to spread the paste on both sides of the strip of jaconette and right down into the joint. Take away the piece of waste paper used for protection and close the book. Do not open it again. After dealing with the other end of the book in the same way, put it between two pressing boards.

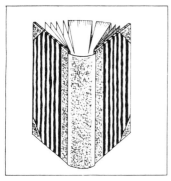

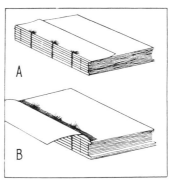

2. The boards must only reach as far as the joints and the book should be pressed for a minute. It must then first be opened up and next laid between two pressing boards. In a day's time it will be dry and ready for the final pressing, lasting 10-12 hours. It is wise to keep glazed paper between the book and the boards to avoid sticking. The book is now ready.

2. They will now lie between the jaconette and the flange. Here you can see the difference between this process and the one previously described.

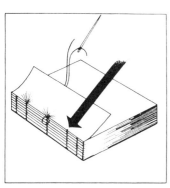

A Heavier Binding
1. This style of binding is sewn in the same way as described earlier. When it is taken out of the sewing frame the frayed cord ends are not pasted to the flange but pulled into it. This is achieved by making holes in the flange and pulling the ends through with a needle and thread, as shown.

3. Next glue the spine, trim the edges and round the spine just as before. The joint will be knocked down somewhat deeper than with the other method. The edges are cut and decorated in the same way.

Lining the Boards
1. After cutting the board for binding the book, line one face of it with paper. Generally newspaper is used. Thin paste is spread on the paper.

Pasting the Boards
1. When the boards are ready to attach to the book, spread paste on each, covering an area somewhat smaller than the flange, as shown here. The paste is applied to the unlined side. If any paste goes on the edge of the board, wipe it off with a finger before it can dry.

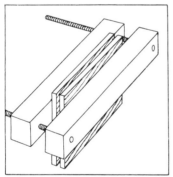

2. After lining, bring the boards together, lined face inwards, and give them a short but heavy press between two pressing boards. Then leave them to lie between two pressing boards drying for a day.

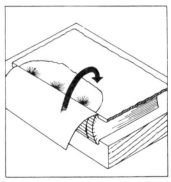

Attaching the Boards
1. Bring one of the boards up to the book and place it so that it lies right against the joint. Paste down the cord ends and press them onto the board, then press the flange onto the paste.

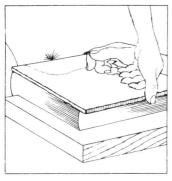

2. To help to force the board right into the joint, pull hard on the cord ends, at the same time pushing the board against the joint. Start with the centre cord.

4. Now lay the book between several sheets of paper and a pair of pressing boards and press it for 10-12 hours.

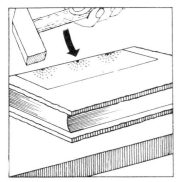

3. After attaching both boards, smooth out any unevenness in the cord ends with a few taps with a hammer.

5. The binding continues with the attachment of the headbands. Spread the spine with thin glue and lay a piece of kraft, as long as the distance between the headbands but 30-40mm (1¼-1½ inches) broader than the spine, along one edge of the spine and bend it across the spine. The part of the kraft which extends beyond the other edge of the spine should be folded back, flattened with a bone folder and cut off with a paper knife.

6. When the book is dry, tear off the unpasted part of the flange and rub down the edge of the flange with sandpaper.

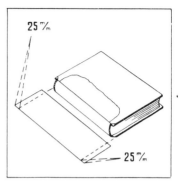

Cutting the Hollow and the Leather

1. Measure the hollow and cut it so that it has the same height as the book, and then cut the leather for the spine and corners. The sizes of these are, as we said earlier, a matter of taste but in the case of the spine 25mm (1 inch) of extra length must be allowed at each end for turning in.

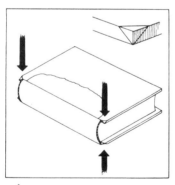

7. Trim the corners of the boards adjacent to the spine with a wedge-shaped cut as shown here.

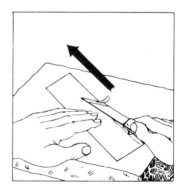

Paring the Leather

1. To ensure a smooth join between the leather and the paper used for the sides of the book, the leather must be pared. To do this the leather is laid on a paring stone with the flesh side uppermost. It should then be pared parallel with the edge.

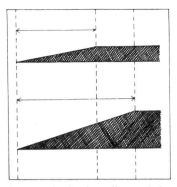

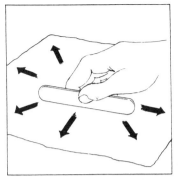

2. Pare the leather all round the edges. As the drawings show, the thicker the leather, the greater the amount which must be pared away. For leather of average thickness, it will be sufficient to pare 5-10mm ($\frac{1}{5}$-$\frac{2}{5}$ inch) off the sides and 25mm (1 inch) off the ends of the spine. The corners are pared most on the side which will be on the face of the covers. Often the material for the corners is pared over its whole surface.

4. If you are using coloured sheepskin leather it must be dampened before it is cut to size and pared. The leather is dipped in water and wrung out in a cloth; after that it is smoothed out with a bone folder with strokes in all directions. You must use a wooden rule for cutting out the material as a metal rule would stain the leather. It must be said that uncoloured sheepskin is a very difficult material to work with.

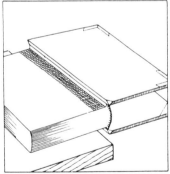

3. The outline of the hollow should be drawn out on the spine leather, after which the leather should be reduced in thickness with a piece of sandpaper at the places where it will cover the joint.

Putting On the Spine and Corners
1. The spine and corners can be pasted at the same time. They are then put aside for about 10 minutes. After that the paste will have soaked into the leather and it must be pasted once more. The corners are put on as previously described and the book is left to dry with the binding open as shown. Leather corners can be attached with glue but for the spine paste is always used.

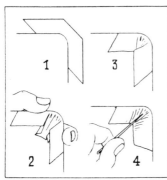

2. Sometimes it is desirable to have rounded corners. Cut each corner with a knife and smooth with sandpaper. Pare the leather over a greater distance than normally. Bend the corner over with two fingers at each edge simultaneously so that the surplus lies under the two turned-in ends. Use a nail to fold the surplus into small pleats. Finally flatten the corner with a hammer.

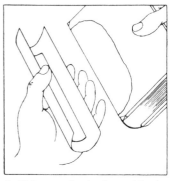

4. Take up the leather with the hollow inside and put the closed book into the spine.

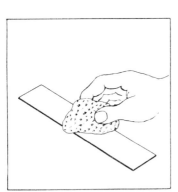

3. Before the spine is covered, the hollow should be moistened with water on the side which is to go next to the leather. It is then put in the middle of the piece of leather which is to be used for the spine. The edges of the hollow can be smoothed with sandpaper before pasting.

5. Turn the book over and press the leather down over the spine with a hand. Take care not to displace the hollow.

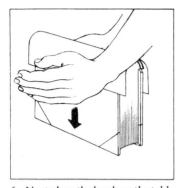

6. Next place the book on the table and press the leather lightly over the spine with the balls of your thumbs, which must be moistened first.

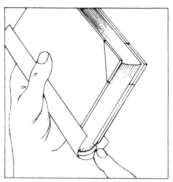

8. When the book has been set aside for about a quarter of an hour, so that the leather can set, fresh paste can be applied and the ends of the spine turned in as explained earlier.

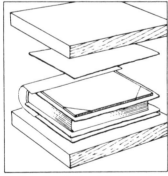

7. Now lay the book between two pressing boards; lay thin board, of the sort used for the hollow, both inside and outside of the cover boards. The purpose of this is to take the dampness out of the leather.

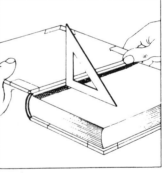

9. Bend the cover open; press the leather onto the cover and the wedge-cut corners. Keep the cover square over the joint during this operation.

10. When the book is closed up, you must press firmly on the turned in parts so that they do not get wrinkled.

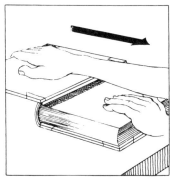

12. After adjusting the head, open the book and pull the covers inwards so that they lie perpendicularly over the joints.

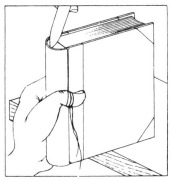

11. Lay a doubled length of thread over the wedge-cut corners and use it to pull the leather in. At the same time press the head out so that the headband follows a regular curve. This is done more easily if you dampen the bone folder with a little water.

13. When the book has been left to dry between two boards for 10-12 hours it is time to finish off the turn in. Open up the book and pare away a piece of the spine leather with a sharp knife as shown. Pare the leather in such a way that it extends 1cm ($\frac{3}{8}$ inch) further in at the outer edge than at the end nearest the contents of the book.

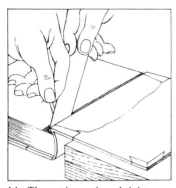

14. The cut is continued right over the edge of the board and all the way down into the joint.

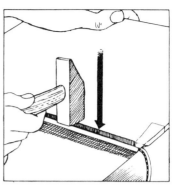

2. When the edge of the cover stands right over the joint, pull the book back against your body and knock the cover down so that it touches the joint along the whole length. Now you are ready to attach the end papers.

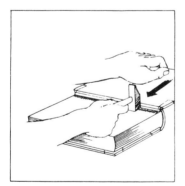

Knocking Down the Covers
1. Dampen the head with a little water to prevent it from cracking, and pull the cover in with the left hand while holding a hammer head against it.

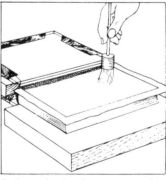

3. Lay the book on a pressing board and bend both covers back. Lay a piece of waste paper under the end paper and spread glue on the end paper and on both sides of the strip of jaconette.

4. Remove the waste paper and lift the end paper up by a finger pressed onto it at each corner. Bend the paper back over towards the cover . . .

6. Then the end paper can be pulled carefully back with the thumbs before being pressed down hard onto the cover.

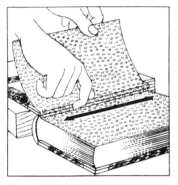

5. . . . but do not yet press down onto the cover; hold at an inclined angle while pressing it well into the joint with the thumb and forefinger.

7. Now lay a piece of paper over the edge of the cover (keeping the cover perpendicular over the joint) and through it press the end paper well down with the fingers. It is very important that the paper is held firmly in place.

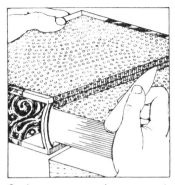

8. As soon as the paper is removed, carefully press the end paper under the lower edge of the cover with a bone folder.

10. When the other end of the book has been finished in the same way, the book must be left open to dry for 30-45 minutes. If the upper cover tends to sink, support it with a piece of board bent in the manner shown here.

9. Give the end paper a final pressing with a finger and a bone folder from the hinge and outwards through a loose piece of waste paper.

11. Now pick up the book with the covers hanging downwards . . .

12. . . . and close the book by holding it in the hands and letting it fall by its own weight onto the cover. Then turn the book over and allow it to fall shut the other way.

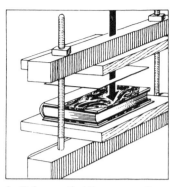

2. Take care that the pressure from the press lies over the fore edge of the book.

Pressing the Book
1. When the book is dry it has to be pressed for 10-12 hours. Put some glazed paper inside the covers (right up to the hinges) and also on the outside of the book.

3. The book is now ready. Check that the binding has been done perfectly by standing the book on its fore edge. If all is well, it will stand perfectly perpendicularly.

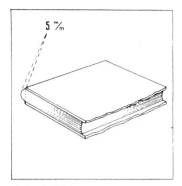

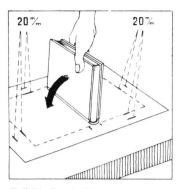

A Book Without a Hollow
1. The book should be cut and rounded. Cut the boards for the sides precisely to the height of the book, spread with glue and put on so that they lie 5-6mm ($\frac{1}{5}$-$\frac{1}{4}$ inch) forward from the spine. Press the book for half an hour. The cloth for the spine should be cut a little higher than the covers and the spine and cloth should both be spread with glue.

Full Binding in Paper, Cloth or Leather
1. If the whole of the book is to be covered in one material, a pattern should first be made in paper. The closed book is then laid on the paper and marks made 20mm ($\frac{3}{4}$ inch) from the edge of the cover and the spine. Then turn the book over onto its other side and repeat the marking.

2. Because there is no hollow, the cloth sticks directly to the spine of the book in this method. The joint between the spine and the covers can be put in with a bone folder if you wish, though this part of the process can be omitted so that no joint is visible. When the book, after being left to dry, receives its final pressing the pressing boards must not lie over the spine, only on the sides of the book.

2. Cut out cloth or leather after drawing in outlines of the book in pencil. Usually paper and cloth are attached with glue, and leather with paste. After the cover material has been glued or pasted the spine should be set in place in line with the pencil marks. The book should be picked up and the side parts of the material folded in so that they will not stick to the boards.

3. Place the book fore edge down on a pressing board and rub down the spine by hand and mark in the joint. Then open one cover and place the book on the table as shown. Pull out the material for the other cover, straighten it and press it onto the board. Then turn the book over and repeat the process for the other cover.

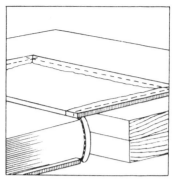

5. Bend down the little points at each corner and hammer them against the edge of the board. Then rub down with a bone folder. Leave the book to dry between two pressing boards. When it is dry trim off the turned in parts and tidy up before attaching the end papers to the boards in the usual way.

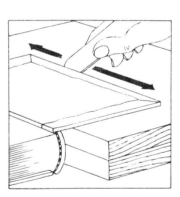

4. Leave the book under light pressure between two pressing boards for half an hour. Cloth and imitation Niger can be protected by placing 5-6 sheets of newspaper between the book and the boards. Apply fresh paste or glue to the parts to be turned in, trim off the corners and beat down the covering material at the spine and at the top and bottom edges of the cover boards.

6. If the full binding is in paper, the book often has concealed cloth corners. Small corner pieces can be put in as described previously. You may trim back the paper so that these corners become visible.

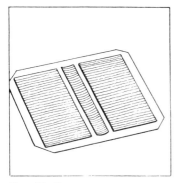

Case Binding

1. All mass produced books with hard covers are bound by the method called case binding, in which the cover is assembled separately and put onto the book as a complete unit. Boards for the sides and a board lining for the spine are laid onto the pasted surface of the cover material. The material is turned in over the boards and the binding is then attached to the book.

Raised Bands

1. On old books the cords were not set into saw cuts so they showed as raised areas across the spine. This effect, called 'raised bands', is often imitated in modern bookbinding. To achieve it, cut a strip from board used for making hollows. The width of the bands is a matter of taste but we suggest 4mm ($\frac{5}{32}$ inch). Then cut the strip into several pieces, each a little longer than the breadth of the spine.

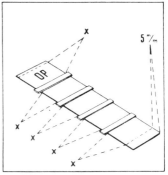

2. Lay these pieces onto the hollow so that the intervals between each pair are equal, except that the distance from the head to the first band should be a little greater while the distance from the foot to the last band should be longer by 5mm ($\frac{1}{5}$ inch).

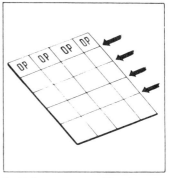

3. If there are several books to be bound in the same way, the hollows can be cut out from one piece of board. The positions for the bands should be marked on the board before the individual hollows are cut apart. Only then can you glue on the bands.

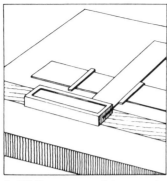

4. While you are gluing on the bands, check with a set square to make sure they are straight. Put the hollow aside to dry between two pressing boards for 5-6 hours.

6. Here are shown some different treatments for raised bands. The device on the last book is cut out from hollow material and glued to the hollow in the same way as the bands.

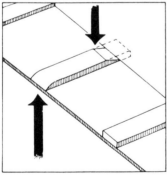

5. When the hollow is dry, cut the bands to the same width as the hollow and then trim the end of each band with a slanting cut. The sharp edges can be rounded off by smoothing them with fine sandpaper.

7. The hollow is put onto the leather spine covering in the usual way before it is attached to the book. Nip the leather well into the bands with your hand or a bone folder. You can also use a piece of cord as shown here.

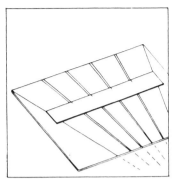

8. To ensure that the raised bands are always correctly positioned, you can make a simple guide from a piece of board. Mark the divisions for the spine along one edge of the board and from there draw lines towards an imaginary centre point in line with the centre line of the board. Put the hollow for the spine on the guide at the place where its head and foot touch the outer lines. Marks can then be made on the hollow to show the correct position of each raised band.

4
DECORATION

This completes the basic processes of bookbinding.
There are, though, various operations concerned with
the decoration of a book which can be used on the
foregoing types of binding, and these are now
described. Since it is the bookbinder's most important
task to harmonize the cover with its contents, it is as
well to be familiar with the ways of decorating the
binding.

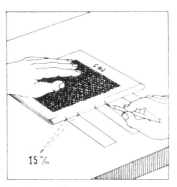

Putting On a Title Label
1. If the leather is such that you cannot apply gold blocking to it, or if you want to show off the title in a different colour, paste or glue on a piece of leather. The title of the book can be written on this label with indian ink or blocked on using tools and gold foil. The leather used for the label must be thin and must be cut out very carefully.

Sewing on Tapes
1. Books which must lie open especially well, such as note books and visitors' books, are often sewn on tapes instead of cords. It is possible to do this form of binding without a sewing frame. First mark the position of the bands on the final end papers . . .

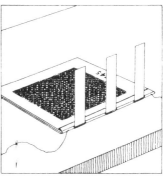

2. A coloured title label is often used on a book bound in patterned paper. The label can be made from book cloth. A label need not only be put on the spine; it can also be attached to the front cover.

2. . . . then bend the tapes in a right angle. Sew through the last section of the book and put the tapes in place before pulling the thread tight. The tapes are now in their correct positions and sewing can continue. Take care not to pull too tightly against the tapes or they may chafe the thread when the book is opened or closed. For this method, of course, it is not necessary to make saw cuts in the sections of the books.

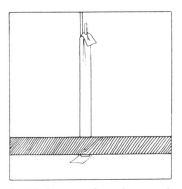

3. It is, however, far easier to work with the tapes on a sewing frame. Fasten the bottom end of each tape with a nail or drawing pin. Cut a small hole in the top of the tape and loop it over the hooks of the frame.

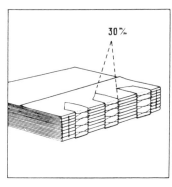

5. When you have finished the sewing, cut the bands off at an angle and glue the ends down to the flange. The book should now be pressed but no joint is knocked in, as it would be impossible to open the book up completely.

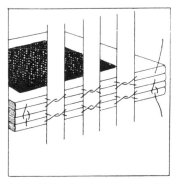

4. A different sewing method is illustrated here; notice how you take the thread down through the thread in the previous section and then up again.

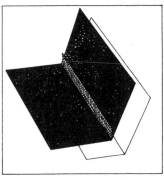

Reinforcing the Joint
1. In books that are used a great deal there is extra wear on the end papers. In such books it helps to add a reinforcement to the joint. A piece of strong cloth is used, in a colour which suits the end paper material. As you make up the end paper, paste the cloth strip onto the coloured face of the end paper, as we show here.

2. After this the book should be bound in the normal way. When the end papers are being pasted to the boards, scratch along the joint with a nail and take off the first page of the end paper. The cloth strip can then be glued to the cover.

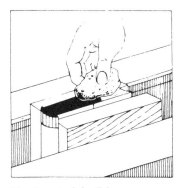

Treatment of the Edges
1. Colouring can be achieved by applying aniline dye to the edge with a small sponge or a wad of cotton wool. Hard, smooth paper which does not absorb moisture is best suited to this treatment. The edge should not have been rubbed with sandpaper. When the colour is dry the edge can be polished by rubbing it with a piece of cloth which has itself first been rubbed with a bit of wax.

3. The sheet of the end paper which was taken away should be trimmed along its edge and then pasted to the cover so that it over-laps by a small amount the strip of cloth.

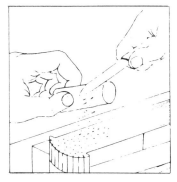

Chalking
1. The edges can be treated with small flakes of ordinary black-board chalk. First dampen the chalk with a little water. After sprinkling the chalk can be brushed off again. Several applications can be made in the same manner and different effects can be achieved by using several colours. Other materials that can be used to treat the edges are: tea-leaves, corn, sand, tobacco, etc.

5
PERFECT BINDING

1. A modern threadless binding process can be used for such works as magazines, handbooks and other publications which did not have sewn bindings in the first place. Using a synthetic glue to hold the pages together it is not necessary to sew the sections together; the glue penetrates a little way into each sheet and the process is called 'perfect binding'. The fore edge of the book is cut as the first step.

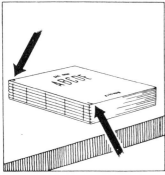

2. The spine should be cut so that the book becomes just a collection of loose sheets.

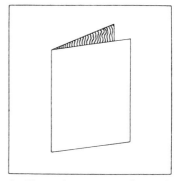

3. The end papers can be made from sheets of paper, folded as shown. No strip of jaconette need be pasted in, nor is a joint formed at the spine. Position the end papers before the first sheet of the text and after the last.

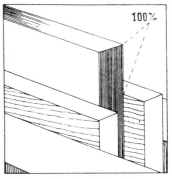

4. Place the book in the press between two pressing boards in such a way that it projects 100mm (4 inches) beyond the edges of the boards. This distance can vary according to the thickness of the book.

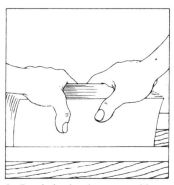

5. Bend the book to one side so that the pages present a staggered face, after which the spine can be spread with glue.

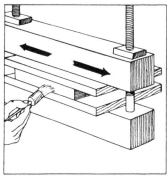

7. Stand the book up so that the spine is perfectly even, then put it back in the press between two pressing boards whose edges are flush with the spine. It is wise to put glazed paper between the book and the boards to protect the boards from glue. Now give the spine a third gluing.

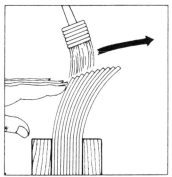

6. As you see, bending the book ensures that the glue attaches to a small edge of each sheet in the book. Next bend the book the other way and apply glue once more.

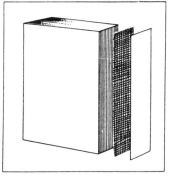

8. While the book is still in the press glue a strip of jaconette to the spine, followed by a piece of paper.

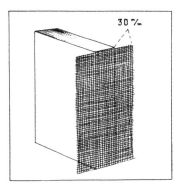

9. Cover the spine of the book with a strip of jaconette which extends 30mm (1¼ inch) beyond the spine on either side. The parts which project are used as flanges and the boards for the cover should be glued to them. The rest of the binding operation continues as described earlier (see page 48).

10. If you want the book to have a rounded spine, press the leaves of the book, after the edges have been cut, against a piece of zinc curved to the desired shape. Then the book is put into the press and the spine glued as already described.

CLEANING AND REPAIR OF BOOKS

Many books, after constant use, need a basic cleaning and sometimes torn pages have to be repaired. In the worst cases a book may have to be taken apart and broken down into its sections, and dust and loose dirt brushed away. Surface spots on soft paper can be removed with crumbs of French bread; on harder paper they can be taken away with an india rubber.

Brown spots can almost always be removed by first putting the section in warm water and then leaving it to dry in sunlight. Bleaching agents such as ammonia water, bleach solution and acid salts can be used but only very well thinned and with great care.

Dirty finger marks can be washed away with soapy water while grease spots can be taken out with benzene or ether, or by pressing the leaf between powdered pipe clay or chalk.

When paper has been soaked through it loses some of its original sizing and this has to be replaced. You can do this by dissolving about 100g (3½oz) size (joiner's glue) in 3.5 litres (6 pints) of warm water with alum; dip the section or sheet into the solution or dab on the solution with a sponge and then hang the section up to dry.

Old and much used books often need patching. For this use the best paper of the same type as that already used in the book. Make sure the thickness, structure and colour are similar. If the colour is not identical it can be altered with thin coffee, tea or aniline dye. Missing corners are best repaired by tearing the edge of the patch so that the overlap is as thin as possible. The grain of the paper must be the same in the patch as it is in the page which is being repaired.

When you are repairing a page in the manner described earlier you must stop the paper curling. This is achieved by dampening both the page to be mended and the paper used for patching before you paste it.

The leather spine covering and corners can be cleaned at the same time by rubbing them with a flannel cloth which has been dipped in a solution of paraffin mixed with twice its own volume of castor oil. Afterwards they are wiped with a soft cloth. Sheepskin can be cleaned with lanolin or olive oil. For general renovation of leather a white shoe-cream is very useful and will remove stains and blotches.

The binding itself may be found to be damaged in various ways:

1. Some or all of the thread can be broken. In this case the book must be taken out of its binding, cleaned and freed from old threads and glue and re-sewn; after that it can be put back in the original cover, provided the cover itself is in reasonable condition.

2. If the jaconette and the end papers are damaged at the joint the book can be repaired by gluing a strip of jaconette over the spine. This jaconette must be wider than the spine by 6cm (2¼ inches), so that there is 3cm (1⅛ inch) to spare on either side of the spine. The book can then be put back into the old cover.

3. If the leather or cloth spine is split on one or both sides it can be put on with a pocket made from kraft (see page 93). If you want to make a stronger job of this repair, you can loosen the leather or cloth a couple of centimetres on either side of the tear and push a piece of well pared leather or cloth under the old material.

4. If the spine leather or the corners are frayed through wear they can be filled out with paste. When the paste is dry it can be cleaned with thinned egg white. The damaged leather can also be given a face-lift by treating it with a mixture of PVA adhesive, alcohol and white shellac. Mix one part of PVA with 3-4 parts of alcohol until it becomes a clear jelly; then add a little white shellac. When this mixture is applied, it solidifies to a transparent film.

5. If the paper covering the sides is damaged, it can be removed after being moistened with tepid water; new paper can then be put on instead. Possibly the end papers may also have to be replaced. The old ones can be loosened and freed with the aid of water.

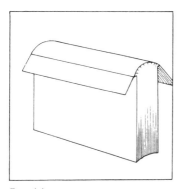

Repairing

1. Often one has books which are damaged or in need of a new binding. In that case it may not always be necessary to re-bind the book completely; it may be possible to effect a simple repair. After taking off the covers and spine, glue a piece of jaconette over the spine of the book with a piece projecting on either side of the joint.

3. If more work is needed, remove the first and last sections, enclose them in new end papers and strips of jaconette and sew them back onto the rest of the book. Then glue jaconette to the spine and replace the binding in the usual way.

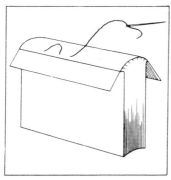

2. The jaconette can be sewn to the spine with a few stitches carefully put into the first and last sections of the book. The cover can be glued to the jaconette, after which the new end papers are put in.

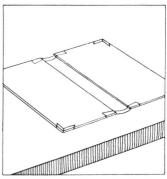

4. A new binding can also be put on with the aid of a pocket. The new binding is made separately so that it is ready to attach to the book.

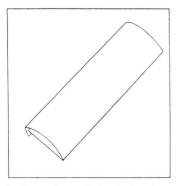

5. Form the pocket out of a piece of kraft, folded as shown so that its breadth is a little less than that of the spine of the book. Glue the pocket together and then . . .

7. After that, glue the hollow to the other side of the pocket and attach the end papers to the book in the normal way.

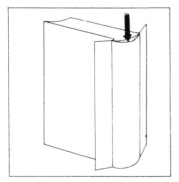

6. . . . . the side which has been glued should itself be glued to the spine.

GLOSSARY

Bank paper Thin, strong white paper.

Baskerville A popular type face, designed in 1756.

Batik A cloth suitable for covering books. The design is produced by coating with wax those parts not to be coloured and dipping the cloth in dye.

Blind Blocking A tooled design produced by stamping on leather without using gold foil.

Blocking Press A small press, heated by electricity, which is sometimes used to impress gold foil designs and lettering on leather or cloth with brass type.

Bodoni Type face designed in about 1790.

Collation Arrangement of pages or sections in their correct order.

Decorating tools Brass shafts with motifs cut into the face. Used to stamp gold designs onto leather or cloth.

Doublure The lining, usually leather, pasted down onto the boards as a separate piece.

Figure The pattern or grain of leather.

Fillets Decorating tools consisting of a brass disc attached by an iron shaft to a wooden handle. The disc is heated and impresses a line on leather. They can be thick or thin and make continuous or broken lines.

Finishing Decoration of a binding —see 'forwarding'.

Folio The format achieved by making one fold in a printed sheet of paper.

Fore Edge The front edge of a book when it stands on end.

Format The shape of a book.

Forwarding The operation of binding a book as opposed to the 'finishing' or decoration. Traditionally the two operations were carried out by different sections of workers in the bindery.

Foxing Brown stains which appear in due course in paper of poor quality.

Full Binding A form of binding where the whole book is covered in one material.

Garamond A type face designed in 1532.

Glaire A medium applied to covering materials so that gold foil will stick to the surface.

Gold foil A thin sheet of plastic or paper coated with metal. Stamping with a hot tool releases the coating of gold and presses it onto the covering material of the book.

Guards Strip of paper or linen used to strengthen the spine of a section.

Half Binding A form of binding where the spine and corners are bound differently from the sides.

Headband A coloured strip of material glued to the head and foot of the spine for decoration.

Jaconette A gauze-like woven cotton used for reinforcing spines and joints.

Linson A toughened paper with patterned surface used for covering books.

Marbled Paper Paper decorated with a pattern, made by laying oil colours on a water base. When the colours are swirled they form the pattern but do not mix. A sheet of paper laid on the surface of the water will take up the pattern.

Morocco Goatskin from North Africa or Cape Town.

Octavo Format resulting from folding a printed sheet three times to give eight sheets and sixteen sides.

Parchment Leather made from sheepskin treated with lime (similar to vellum which comes from calfskin).

Perfect Binding A method of binding where the spine of the book is coated with a flexible PVA glue to hold individual sheets in place.

Pigskin A good hard-wearing leather for covering books.

Quarter Binding A form of binding where the spine is covered with a different material from the rest of the book.

Quarto The format resulting when a sheet is folded once (folio) and then a second time to give four sheets or eight sides.

Raised Bands Bands across the spine of a book. Formerly these bands were the cords which supported the threads binding the sections of the book. Now they are false and form a way of decorating the spine.

Russian Leather Calfskin treated with birch oil.

Section A collection of pages resulting from a printed sheet being folded several times to give many pages.

Shagreen Goatskin from the East Indies.

Signature The key printed in small type at the foot of the first page in a section to identify it and show its place in the book.

Tip In Attaching a leaf to another with a thin strip of glue. Used for binding single sheet illustrations, maps etc.

Vellum Leather made from calfskin treated with lime (similar to parchment which is sheepskin).

FURTHER READING

There are quite a number of books available in bookshops and libraries but one of the best and most comprehensive is *The Thames and Hudson Manual of Bookbinding* by Arthur W. Johnson—Thames and Hudson, London 1978.

WHERE TO BUY MATERIALS

Dryad Limited, PO Box 38, Northgates, Leicester.
Reeves & Sons, 178 High Street, Kensington, London W8.
Russell Bookcrafts, Bancroft, Hitchin, Hertfordshire.